RINGER

Pitt Poetry Series

Ed Ochester, Editor

RINGER

Rebecca Lehmann

University of Pittsburgh Press

This book is the winner of the 2018 Donald Hall Prize for Poetry, awarded by the Association of Writers and Writing Programs (AWP). AWP, a national organization serving more than three hundred colleges and universities, has its headquarters at George Mason University, Mail Stop 1E3, Fairfax, VA 22030.

The Donald Hall Prize for Poetry is made possible by the generous support of Amazon.com.

Published by the University of Pittsburgh Press, Pittsburgh, Pa., 15260

ISBN 13: 978-0-8229-6595-4
ISBN 10: 0-8229-6595-X

Cover art: *Sadie and the Birdcage, 2013,* by Cig Harvey
Cover design: Melissa Dias-Mandoly

for Asa Walter

It's no accident: women take after birds and robbers just as robbers take after women and birds.

—HÉLÈNE CIXOUS, "THE LAUGH OF THE MEDUSA"

CONTENTS

Two

THREE

RINGER

Natural History

Tell me the world. Here comes light, unspoken.
Light hooks a claw on the horizon, pulls itself
into view. Here comes water, saline,
scattering single-celled organisms.
Land is a puppet. It climbs hydrothermal vents like stairs.
Lava congeals. Land rises. Here comes land,
hand-springing out of water. Wind is a comma,
pausing the day. At night, wind kicks its legs.
What about multi-celled life? What about invertebrates
and vertebrates? Tell me evolution.
Tell me old growth forests. Tell me a rainbow.
Tell me blue-tailed skinks. Here comes science,
explaining eyeballs. Look, here come the stars.
Here comes a commuter train, hopping the rails
and crashing into an empty sidewalk
at 2:30 in the morning. Here come sparklers.
Use them to trace letters of light in the darkness.
Here comes someone's childhood cat. Here comes a paper
about George Washington, complete with colored
pencil illustrations of his many sets of false teeth.
Tell me bourgeois glass lanterns strung from a live oak.
Tell me a graveyard bigger than its town.
Please understand I mean no harm. Hold the phone.
Here comes Tina, hand-springing across the backyard.
Here comes a tent. Wind boxes its nylon sides,
scaring the children, their sleeping bags unfurled
and arranged like daisy petals. Tell me a flashlight.

ONE

RINGER

Each morning trumpeted into being with a chorus of baby squawks.
Daffodils pushed through the barely revealed spring mud. Crusted snow
clung to the curbs. In his crib, my infant son sucked his fist
until he gagged. The polka dot mesh crib bumper that we painstakingly
selected surrounded him. In the afternoons, I pushed the stroller around
the block and around the block again, taking note of the finely painted
Victorian homes, each so full of wood, waiting to be undone
by one errant spark from a frayed electric wire. I pushed the stroller
around the block again. I put the baby in a snowsuit that made
him look like a bear. The neighborhood nodded its approval.
We left winter behind. My infant son smiled in my arms.
Spring opened up to us, the days stretching like the baby himself
in his crib after his morning nap. I was not on the couch crying.
Who knew how the afternoon would unfold? I put the baby down
for a nap. I cradled the baby in a creaky wooden rocker.
I held the baby in my arms. He smiled. He bounced his open mouth
against my shoulder. We lay on the living room floor, he on his play mat,
me on the rug, listening to Joni Mitchell: *O star light, star bright,*
you've got the lovin' that I like all right / Turn this crazy bird around.
I walked the baby around the block in the stroller. The clouds nodded
their approval, let fly a short frenzy of final snowflakes that glistened
in the afternoon sun. The baby quaked his clenched fists. I put the baby
in a vibrating chair that rocked back and forth and played electronic lullabies.
Why is the bumblebee yellow and black? Why does the snow recede
from the back porch like waves of sadness? The tulips poked up
through the dead earth not unlike the tulips stitched into the decorative quilt
that hung above the hospital bed where I gave birth. There, two medical students
held my legs and joked about going to the gym. The epidural coursed
strong medicine into my spine. The anesthesiologist flitted in
and out of the room like a large hummingbird. Finally, I held the baby
in my arms. He opened his eyes. His eyes were all the hung-over mornings
I'd forgotten, every drunken sunrise I'd slept through. His eyes
were four dozen Canadian geese lifting off a late summer river, all at once.

AMOEBAE

This is a poem about telling the truth.
Don't look for love here. You won't find it.
You'll find the night, crusted with galaxies,
hitching above the unturned chevrons of my house.
You'll find a mouse curled in a ball in the wall
next to an unchewed electrical wire.
The mouse is not playful. When I talk,
no one listens. I walk through the dark
of the house breathing out moist vowels.
Upstairs, my son pretends at sleep in his crib.
His baby teeth calcify into lumps in his jaw,
push against the insides of his gums.
His thumb, slippery with spit beside his mouth,
twitches only once. Meanwhile, snails
ravage the garden. The last of the pumpkin
blossoms fold in on themselves, unsexed
and heavy with powdery mildew.
In the artificial light of the dining room,
I cut pictures of the baby into circles
and stars, paste them onto the nautically themed
pages of his keepsake book. Each snip
of the scissors punctuates the unleavened night.

Say the night is loneliness. It's not.
It's the thoughtless night. Nor am I white-
hearted Atropos. In the basement,
the cistern crackles with spiderwebs and dust.
I do not place a handful pennies there
and return to find a pitcher full of ocean water.
Inside the water, only amoebae and unrehearsed light.

MORNING LASSO

Morning wandered into the middle of the road.
You're right. Stop reading. I was driving you to work.
Morning occluded sound and light. Morning
chokeholded the roadside. The wind sheered
all memory of roses. The wind sheered the metal
sheet laid atop a pothole. Morning dilated.
Morning faked an ocular migraine. Cancel story.
Morning wants to sex you up. Morning sneaks.
Cancel roses. Morning couldn't summarize the night.
Cancel circumcised light. Alright. Send sparrows.
It was all a mistake and I'm not a woman.
Expectant morning scrubbed daylight. Locked-down
and berserk, morning fussed and buckled.
Morning's pupils incinerated the road. We internalized
the stoic countryside. Morning came pronouncing
and freckled, heckling sooty snow banks. The foothills
gave up. Morning somersaulted, musky and forceful.
Line morning with collected geodes. Line it
with the finger paintings of privileged children.
Morning wasn't even one of us. Morning's split
lip leaked out a universe. Orbiting one of those stars,
at least for now, we exist. Morning wandered into
the middle of the road. You're right. Stop reading.

CORKER

Held between ice-sheathed car in the driveway
and sticky fingers of daycare dropoff,
between frozen car locks in the airport parking lot,
and kiss with tongue by the carousel at the mall,
this moment, this morning. I walk back from here.

How I reversed the "less than" sign on the chalk board,
and the math professor auditing my class corrected me.
How I kept conflating words after the concussion,
replacing *sugar* with *silence* and *ticket* with *tragic*,
as in, "Please pass me the silence," and, "I misplaced my tragic."

I went to the conference. I took a long flight.
I suffered a sinus infection. I took strong antibiotics
and slept alone in an airport hotel room under a thick comforter.
I tended to the chapped and reddened butt of a toddler,
my own son, after the diarrhea he got from
the medicine for an ear infection.

I stood in the middle of the airport thinking about
how one day it would be leveled down to its foundation,
a ruin of 21st Century America, how all the people in it
would die and mostly be forgotten, how I might be witnessing
the decline of America. See: the Make America Great Again hats
stacked in a red pyramid on the souvenir cart outside security;
the president at the press conference telling a reporter his question
is stupid, to sit down, be quiet; the poem a 4th grader submitted
to the community outreach program I run that read,
"I hope that Donald Trump can Make America Great Again /
I hope that Mexicans don't steal are jobs."

There is rent. There are bills. There are groceries to buy.
There is my husband. There is the dour Northeast—
all the snow, and nobody ever smiling. There is our son,
resplendent toddler learning the alphabet and numbers
and how to go on the potty, who tells me again and again,
"Daddy cleaned Asa's poop off carpet."

There is the pregnancy I lost last fall, the cavernous grief
that swallowed me, swallowed me.
Hold my hand. Would you like to go upstairs?
There are my son's hazel eyes, browning now near the pupils, like mine.
Look, here are the airline seats. Here is gravity.
We could be floating in the cabin with the pretzel packs
and cans of juice, but we're not.

One brazen bird calls outside the window.
I don't know what kind. It's February,
almost spring. It's been snowing for days,
until now, the sun glinting off a three foot drift,
melting its surface ever so slightly, and, beneath it,
evenly spaced in frozen dirt, the crocus bulbs I planted
in grief last October, waiting to crack open into beauty.

SWERVE

Alright, be the columns of the abandoned sanitarium, high up in the mountains.
Be the copper kettle left in the industrial kitchen.
Be the spider webs enveloping the cracked milk house glass windows.
Be the snowcapped air. Be the mineral water filling the great outdoor pool
where once the wealthy patients stretched and glided.
Be the tulips we drive by, losing their petals.
How do you know I hate the night? Be the church parking lot
filled with motorcycles. Really? How do you know I hate
each fine spring day, high up in the mountains? Be an A-frame house
sequestered amongst the pines. Be the weather, the true protagonist
of the novella the car is writing as we drive through the mountains.
O the crabapple blossoms, the cherry blossoms, the tri-colored lilacs,
their petals cascading, cascading down upon the sidewalks
high up in the mountains. Be the original town, not the part of town
made to look like an Alpine village for Canadian tourists. Look, it was morning.
Fuck that. Be the ecstatic middle night. Be the light through yonder window.
Soft, be the lilac branch breaking. Darling, be the mountains. Be the snow
that has almost completely melted off of them. Be the rough mortar between
the stones of the well, behind the old church in the village, high up
in the mountains. Be the aging man in a green sweater leaning
over the well's edge. Be the infinite dark of water dropping down inside.
Be the cool smell of the wet moss carpeting the well's slick mouth.
How do you know I hate the aging man? How do you know I hate the cliffs,
behind the well, behind the church? How do you know I hate the mountains?
Be the rocks threatening to fall off the cliffs, onto the highway
we are driving on, high up in the mountains. Be the car's slow swagger.

TIME TRAVELER

I regard myself with utmost suspicion.
This is what I did: I hollowed
out a decorative gourd; I made
a soup out of animal parts
and green vegetables. There's no
predetermination. Don't go outside
at dusk or dawn. Even a queen
can be beheaded. So Anne Boleyn,
and the executioner from Calais,
the swift reflection of his sword.
I'm a real person. Am I a real person?
Time is a form, an envelope fat
with discarded grocery lists,
an overdue bath. Both beaches
and tar soaked gravel roads
operate under the rule of direction.
To avoid contamination: wear
long pants; drain standing water;
carry an ornate paper lantern
in the dark. Recall the carnival ride
that spins rapidly and pins the rider
to its walls as the floor falls away.
As if drawn to scale, each part
of the day, meticulously shaded,
accumulates. Each second threatens
to capsize time. Large planes sprayed
DDT on the northern counties.
The wonder rung like sunshine
on a winter afternoon. But it wasn't
winter. Every moment is the most
modern moment possible. The herbs
collected from the remnant garden
were waxy and tasted like regret.
And the starlings flying into swarms
above the highway—the twisting
and turning of the cloud of wings,
a wrist-flicked neck-break of feathers.

RIVER

You wanted the violence of women against you.
Women, rough and tumble as burdens, burned across
the open fields that turn and un-helix parched wind.
Women, whose feet cramp in the night, buried in blankets
piled high as tire fires. Does god love us? Dunno.
But you wanted the softness of women against you,
bodies that make other bodies, muffled and sweaty.
Softness was a duffel bag full of knives stashed
in the back of the pantry. Softness was a chapped nipple.
You wanted broad sad bitches against your head
like an electric storm. You colored the women
nightshade blue. They sunk to the bottom of the river.
The riverstones roughed the women up, like you wanted to.
Like you wanted to, the current choked them, pulled
their hair, banged their skulls into the river bed,
pushed their faces into pillows of silt. There's no lower place.

The world is an old grave. Women sparkle like cheap
glitter from its bottom. There's permanence in lying.
Like how glass is a liquid pretending to be a solid.
Like how watching the world from the bottom of a river
is like looking out a window in an abandoned house,
waiting for a slipstream to chisel the sky into ripples.

SEAS, SILVER

From the bridge, our captain, stolid in her green wool coat,
taxies our ship. We eek past the shaggy pines on shore.
Pretend to be the microwave, abandoned overboard,
its door swung open. From the bridge, our captain smells
of wet wool—itchy, itchy. Be kind to the soft flesh of her body.
Her fingernails puncture light. Are we losing speed?
Our captain holds course. She circumnavigates the island.
The crew: an amalgamation of Mylar blankets
and balaclavas.
                What if we sung her name? Winter is a fable.
What did we know of ravenous equinoctial light? Unhook day
from the cold jaw of the ship. It drags a skulk of unblossomed
hours. The captain loses her tempo. The ship pitches
and yaws. Then winter, a drugged fawn stumbling
through the shaggy pines. We see it from the bulwark.

SNAKES AND THE DARK

Hot, the air from the woodstove
    you open
        to heave in another dried log.
What a bunch of whispered kindling,
    you think,
        that snickers
likes rumors.

        Outside, the spring leaves bud,
          thick like Play-Doh.
    And what pinecones,
        dressing the top lusty
          boughs of the forest,
  that bow in the storm.
        What seraphim.
          What flaming swords.

    Oh sure the trees
  are full of snakes,
      that cover the knotty bark
of their trunks.
      Ignore that.

This is the northern-most county
  of New York state,
      and you're one more
unwashed customer,
    hair stinking
of wood smoke, standing in line
    at the IGA to buy
a 20-pound bag of rock salt.

    There goes your neighbor, flying overhead
      in a plane
    he built in his basement,
      and carried out,
        piece by piece,
      through the cellar doors.

Once, exploding stars shook
             the night's ruby soul
      from its gasping throat.

             Not even I believe that.

LOCKER ROOM TALK

In one hand he held the pussy, and the pussy was moist.
With one hand he hooked the pussy. Did his chubby
hairy ring finger slip inside? Just for a second.
He was careful not to lose his wedding band
up there. Really the pussy should have been
better tended. It stunk like old cod, alewives,
salmon, tuna, whitefish, rotten trout, small mouth
bass, a bucket of putrid lobsters, the bottom
of the Mariana Trench, pickled herring, the skin
behind a dead woman's ear. The pussy was
such a miserable cunt. The pussy was a whore,
a slut, had clearly been finger-banged,
was common property, was hiding a wire
coat hanger. The pussy was relaxing in a bathtub.
It was a little bit bloody. He knew what the pussy
was doing in there, and it was disgusting.
Yes, there should be some punishment for the pussy.
He spanked the pussy. He dug his fingernails in.
He hadn't even bothered to trim them.
He wanted to feel the pussy spasm in his hand,
like the heart of a rabbit bleeding out in the snow.
The pussy was too hairy. Have some decency.
The pussy was a hot piece of ass. The pussy
was a ten. The pussy was a four. Look at that pussy.
Would anyone vote for that? Can you imagine that,
the pussy of our next president? The pussy walks
in front of him, you know? And when the pussy
walked in front of him, believe me, he wasn't impressed.

MAN

Day-born, man springs into the demarcated forest,
into the carpeted suburban home, into the wireless ether
where no wilderness endures. The heft of man
moors him, prevents his gravity-defying buildings
from caving in. He coalesces—goodbye old
civility—not a doddering gentleman, not overly courteous
and backed against the freshly painted wainscoting.
Man claims his post as arbiter of social strata.
He metes out sun-bleached validity. He is not effete.
He wants a wife to wash his weathered winter jacket,
to watch his wayward wend through hill and vale.
He does not forage. The performance of man
never commenced, is not teleological. See man posed
at vertiginous heights. He does not wobble.
No room for man to buy bric-a-brac statues
of big-headed children kissing or jumping rope.
No room for man to travel from wonder to satisfaction,
from satisfaction to calamity. No room for sly
perturbations of ways of knowing or being.
Inject a dead virus into man's arm. The injection site
puckers in the shape of a galaxy. Here is man, apart.
Here is man, alone in silhouette against a window
too large for its wall. Man made it that way on purpose.
Outside the window, a mourning dove builds her nest
in the top of a chimney. Her laments don't resonate
in man's domain. Man's porkpie hat settles just so atop
his short-cropped hair. O golden ratio! O lost poem
of the quintessential sea adventure! O shut man's mouth.

We Got Stuck in a Colonial Painting

Peel away the snowfall like pioneer women in Maine. We got stuck
in a tempest, in a painting of slow colonialism. Were the women
wearing gingham skirts? Tomorrow's a color elegy for the departed ships
and shirtless mermaids sporting big bang-me eyes. Stay grounded.
Push the wind. The early morning flapped against the colonial house
like a forgotten-open storm door. We needed some screws.
Settle tomorrow's broken-winged, symbolic bird. Find remnants
of vacated colonialism. You were already a settler. The insistent
painting pulled me out of bed. Tomorrow's the wind. Get color,
slowly departing the trade ships in the painted storm. Color the porch,
the rain-warped chair anchored to it. Tomorrow's an elegy
for insistent bangs. Screw the wind to the broken bird
carved from wood. You were already an errant ship in Maine.
You were already colonialism. You were already the vacated
Eastern seaboard. Tomorrow's an elegy for gingham skirts.
Tomorrow's a chair screwed to a wall. Push the grounded
early morning against the broken, bang-bang house. We got stuck
in a colonial village. Tomorrow's an elegy for bedded settlers.
You were already screwing the morning. You were already
the snow's insistent dinghy. Were the women wearing velvet skirts?
Color the gingham ships peeling the inconsistent wind.
Color the banged pioneer women crowning the eulogized seaboard.
Tomorrow's an elegy for unmoored porches. Tomorrow's ten pioneer
women in Maine banging a broken storm door. Color the big-
eyed ring of the anchor. Tomorrow's two pointed flukes.
Push the broken tempest against the already departed ship.
Color the insistent women chain gray. Were the panting mermaids
azure and deep-sea fuchsia? Tomorrow's the screwed wing
of a broken storm. We got stuck in an un-shirted, panting wind.
Tomorrow's a sunken shank. Tomorrow's a pioneer anchor
tanking remnant flaps of peeled women. Tomorrow's a vacated skirt.
You were already a broken harpoon. You were already the anchor's crown.

TIME TRAVELER

The stark coos of pigeons nesting
in the attic crowded the morning
like undervalued skill-sets. I de-wormed
the animals, following the directions
on the medication packaging. Compulsive
repetitions constituted my psyche.
The star etched into the frosted glass
in the center of my front door
wasn't part of a larger constellation,
or a constellation of meanings,
a compulsory chain of signifiers.
Look at the crash-and-burn debris
on the side of the road: one leather boot
that's been biodegrading since August.
Its decorative fringe waves lost carbon
into the air. Even after I recollected,
even after *even* fell out of common parlance,
the class "woman" rose up, even-Steven,
and assumed their hoop-skirted places
in the new millennium. At the Ironic Gallery,
the round table sewn from baby-bonnets
served as an example of Exalted Art
of the Everyday. Institute morning.
Institute the bad copy. Institute *even*.
I applied white paint to the baseboards.
I purchased tchotchkes in the shape of owls
and lined them up in the window sills,
hoping they'd attract the real thing,
the genuine article, the whole enchilada.
Through time I heard the call: *Who cooks*
for you? Who cooks for you? Not the lost husband,
that even-handed space-master. Even still,
hand me the nail gun and plywood.
I stand in silhouette at the window,
the clouds of the storm evenly approaching.
There is nobody else here. The washing
machine shudders in the other room.

ACADEMIA

Shut it down. Your day won't come.
For sure, your anger is a hungry spit
of dogs, pulling their chains taut.
But no, ho, lo, what art, what artifice.
Stop it. There's no room for that here.

They can't take this hour away from you,
brown-eyed-Susans lolling in the back-
yard, the gladioli you couldn't tend to,
your son crying over a toy puppy
in the daycare toddler room
with a woman he just met this morning.

Your impertinence, duly noted in a bureaucrat's
fat file of printed out emails.
His smug signature: *We strive for a campus*
that is polite, professional, productive and free from
harassment and discrimination.
The politesse of the situation:
Ignore the White Nationalist student
who wrote a poem about your pussy
getting wet as you lectured
on White Privilege.
She is no real threat.

For sure, she is not stuffing a loaded pistol
into her glovebox as she drives
to campus for the disciplinary hearing.
For sure, you are not worth
the paper your teaching contract
was printed on. There is the student,
by the bathroom, her head shaved,
her stack of evidence about how
her Whiteness isn't being respected.

Go ahead, look her in the eye, that is just
an eye, and not like any other thing,
not like a sour candy, not like
the greedy sun, not like the clarion
ring of a single dead-metal bell.

PORTAL

Dear Reader, night is full of dying brothers.
Your mind: a catacomb of misplaced electrons.
Please bite the plastic paddle. You won't
feel a thing, such as evening, the bathtub
filled with splashing toddler, the steam
from the water fogging the window above it,
washcloth clamped between your chapped lips.
Reader, imagine you courted the full-bodied wind.
What about the lottery of mowed grass and dappled sky?
It's late morning, Reader. Put your shit kickers on.
Get after the buffet of Technicolor farm fields
wrapped as a scarf around a doorknob.
Rejoice: a Family Dollar anchors every town.
Reader, do you even know what a Family Dollar is?
Can you imagine me in one, shopping for babyfood
between two Amish women waiting
for the Adirondack Trailways bus, their makeup-less
faces shadowed by puckered black bonnets?
Reader, cut the barn from the pastel painting
hanging in my hall. Use a pair of safety scissors.
Catch your reflection in the living room window,
your hair snarled, toes chilly. Then, go watch TV.
In the spelunking documentary, darkness saturates
the caves lacing the Mississippi's soggy banks.
Imagine we are lost in one of them, only a candle
to corroborate our frenzied search for a yawning portal
into daylight. Bats snuggle the scalloped drip line.
Albino newts slide across the surface
of a subterranean lake, little winks of marrow.
Love, love. Yes, I see you. Don't fall in there.

Aubade

Once, white roses bracketed the dawn.
Then, Adirondack firs collided

with the day. So the fox became
the hot knife that sliced the forest.

Open the antique shaker cabinet.
The stars become the snow's icy skin.

I think of you as evergreens, as the day's heat.
Collect days as loose sheets of paper,

as iced over storm windows,
as Calliope's iridescent beaches.

Collect pale tongues as the night
is a handful of dead wasps clustered

around the door to the basement.
In the house you don't own,

night clambers in drunk,
impetuous roommate chained to Polaris,

fixed sweet and ready to implode.
Come deciduous morning,

you will arrive, but the peonies
will be snowdrifts. The snowdrifts

will be cool sloughed skin in the bathtub,
the white of the bathtub's acrylic,

the hibernating groundhog's
gentle teeth resting inside her lips,

the telescopic lens of bright day.

PRISM

The baby is a welter of yellow crocuses erupting across the front lawn.
Look away from them. Regard the purple petals superimposed
on the backs of your eyelids. The baby is the neighbor's cat,
slinking outside to sunbathe on the sidewalk. The baby is the afternoon.
The baby shifts in his crib, sucks his fingers, grunts.
The baby is the misplaced folder on a cluttered desk.
The baby is a three-minute phone message about genealogical research
from somebody who thinks they've called the library.
The baby is gender neutral. Let me do it myself.
Grasp spring firmly, as a person coming out of deep sleep
grasps a glass of cool water on the bedside table.
Look, said the voice in the phone message, I'm just trying
to save some money. The baby is Shakespeare's 18th sonnet.
The baby is rough winds. The baby is a stack of discount blue jeans
in the department store. I try on three pairs in the dressing room.
The baby whimpers in his stroller. The baby is a bag of sunflower seeds
resting on the front porch. The baby blows the treetops hither, hither.
Watch the baby flex his fingers, fold them over into fists.
In one arm, I hold the baby, finally able to support his own head.
The baby is all forehead, splotched red from crying.
Is your baby in a bear suit? asks a little girl through the fence.
Her face is smeared with chocolate. The baby is the fence.
The baby is the ball kicked over. The baby curls his toes
around the sun. The sun breaks into rainbows
through the beveled glass. Is your baby sleeping?
What is hegemony? It was always already nap time.
The baby is a tube of blue mascara. The baby is a floppy sun bonnet.
The baby is three Amish houses in a row on a country road.
The baby is three sets of disconnected power lines.
Begin again. The baby is the church bell gonging out each hour.
The children in the daycare play yard shriek behind the fence.

VERSES

The house holds the heat
                  of the day
in its hand like a bee, the evening a mirror
that tethers its streaks
              like the dog
that your mother once bought you
                      who slipped
through the propped open window and shot
like a star in the night.
              You gathered
your courage to find him
                  like daisies in June.

Your mother asks too many questions,
I tell you. My hand by your heart,
                  pitter-pat,
pitter-pat.
           Go sing me some honey-dipped
verses. The forest is golden and flares.

              Your heart
turns the wheel that the forest was built on,
its leaves mirrored secrets
            that button the air.

The air is a fortune we frittered,
                our baby asleep
in his crib, dreaming
          our bones away.

Exit Interview

Thank you for completing night's survey.
Your valued opinions ring across
a thousand fiber optic cables,
buried in semi-frozen ground.
Hear your valued opinions in
the clicking of jawbone on cartilage,
of cartilage on flowering memory.
The student wanted to make you feel the way
she did, bullets tangled in her esophagus.
The wind is a death threat slid
beneath your colleague's office door.
The wind is subzero. The wind can't name
the barrels brushing your hair.
As in the gun dropped
in the college quad, safety off.
As in the whiz of featureless grass
under unbound feet. As in your son
crying on the nursery floor,
the campus daycare worker too frantic
to stop and rub his aching gums.
He wants to be carried to the window,
so he can look at the swallows
in the sightless trees. Such a common bird,
dirty feathered, host to parasites.

Other comments or opinions?
To run, both hands empty,
through the parking lot,
imagining the muzzle at your back.
There is nothing left to say, OK?
Cc: nobody. Bcc: night's bullet-hole stars.

TWO

TWO DEBTORS

Calculate me down to nothing, no numbers,
two null sets for eyes. Then tick back past zero.

Crack open the wack odometer and cheat
it into negatives, reversed image, upside down

and mirrored, slack land of minus. The river
of figures flows north, and we ride its shaky ferry,

never with Charon, but with your mother. See,
I'm always inventing someone to take with me.

Maybe I'm alone on the ferry, which is really
a rickety raft. The blossoms on the trees invert,

swell into no fruit, no thin periwinkle skin,
no moist rosy flesh, all ash. I scratch my back

with a denuded stick. Even my blood's impounded.
The wind's a deflated cactus. The twilight, not full

of milky vespers whispered over paper-skirted
candles held in penitent hands. There's a hole

in my bucket. Out pour wooden nickels.
There's a lien on every broke mouthful of air

I breathe, my hair shivered platinum, my fingers
fat receptacles of emptiness, bankrupt as

the cloudless sky, waiting for a silver heron.

The Beauties

So bare, the bulb of the old man's bathroom, turned on.
The light is the fright of all your childhood dreams.
As in the tent, pitched in the machine shed,
sleeping bag spread, a sloppy camp over gravel,
the smell of oil-soaked rags in an empty plastic
ice cream bucket, "La Bamba" playing on the radio

you want to turn off, but can't reach. So curious,
your child-mind's eye, searching for rainbow-sleeved wind,
invisible in the obsidian night. Your father waits inside
the little house, drinking a Heineken and playing cribbage
with the old man, who is and isn't your grandfather,
the widower, the veteran, missing half his teeth,

fluent also in German, a language he only speaks
to angel-ed time, in the middle of the night,
when the owl's beak blooms open to reveal the ridges
of its probing, clicking tongue, the tuft of mouse fur
stuck to the back of its throat. So the folding chair
propped against the unpainted drywall

of the old man's kitchen, star pattern
punched into its metal seat, onto which, in the morning,
ears ringing with loneliness, you will throw up,
wiping your mouth on the cuff of your pink
unicorn sweatshirt. So the pulsed-out morning star,
daft planet twinkling an empty song. And the carnival

of hoarfrost, striating the autumn-stiff dry prairie grasses
in the field behind the shed. Hello seven sisters
sewn into night's receding sky, puckered and hooked
as the fibers of a soft cream carpet a baby might shove
his weighty fist into, drool cascading, a viscous cataract,
from his swooping lower gum. There will be no

morning-blue flowers to vine you away to a secret
walled garden, no woman to feather you into her arms,
kiss your clammy forehead, comb the tangled fever
from your hair, murmur *Shall I compare thee to a summer's day?*
Thou art more lovely and more temperate, her lips
strawberry red, her breath warm sweetened milk.

DREAMING OF MANGOES

Somewhere a poem is in a heart,
which is to say somewhere a poem is in
a hand-held tape recorder, which is
to say somewhere a poem is in
a pencil sharpener, or a hard hat.
Somewhere a cow's heart is in a thick
stew with finely sliced golden beets
bobbing in the broth like life preservers.
Almost everywhere, life preservers
are tied to the sides of boats: the gargantuan
yachts of the uber-wealthy; shrimp boats
with insect leg masts and nets, matriculating
down river deltas to the gulf; tiny, erect
speed boats zipping and zagging around
the coastlines of the Great Lakes.
Life preservers stare from their sides,
unblinking, un-pupiled eyes. In winter,
on Cape Cod, seagulls peck at the eyes
of dolphins who swim off course and beach
in frigid sand. Somewhere a seagull is lining
a nest with the glass-clear corneas of dozens
of dolphins. Even the nest is an imagined
thing, and nothing like a human brain.
In the nest of the brain, clutter predominates:
calculations of the cost of commuting given
rising fuel prices; a song by the dead
soul singer whose face haunts the TV
all night; a memory of an aunt's mountainous
breasts in a red bikini, her sour peppermint
breath, her long painted fingernails popping
a yellow balloon effortlessly at a cousin's
summer birthday party. Somewhere a red
bikini top holds a string of memories together.
A dolphin is not the same as a memory,
even with its eyes intact. Somewhere,
right now, a dolphin is raping another dolphin,
whose heart undulates like the see-through-
plastic-sac of a jellyfish's long skirt.

On shore, a child in a swim diaper traces
a heart in the sand with her finger.
She is dreaming of sliced mangoes.

THE SEA

Blame me for ebbing, for the printed currents
lisping beneath my spangled apron. I was the ladder

and I was the fall from the ladder, my rough chop
the stitches in your tender scalp. All my anemones

caressed aseptic reason, their multitudinous neon
phalanges prayerful and repressed. Like lightning-struck

trees' covetous tops, my deepest trenches split.
In their biblical darkness, I imagined dozens of rabbits

gliding blithely, as through tall prairie grasses on a hot
dry day in Nebraska. Off tempo and out of key,

I kicked and hit, massaging the needy sandstone
cliffs of this or that coastline. My paint chip waves

crested and crumbled. No soggy horn could counterfeit
my gold-toothed fog, my California tan, the freshwater

slicks of my ice sheets, the brine-sharpened bows
of my sunken ships. Now you see Atlantis, my own

husband, synaptic in the high noon sun.
Now you don't.

EPITHALAMION

When I was a girl in Wisconsin, I dreamed I'd marry
a man from Michigan. Then I did. When I was a man
from Michigan, I dreamed I'd marry a begonia,
flowers choked with pollen. When I was a flower
from Michigan, I dreamed I'd marry a comet
swooping around Jupiter, warming as it
hurtled toward Mars, growing a slick ice tail.
Remember Roethke's boyhood in Michigan,
all the bogs and swamps and German ladies
pruning roses in hothouses while Midwestern
snows settled on dormant backyards?
When I was the snows of Michigan,
I dreamed I married a hothouse.
Remember the snap of the branch
in the dark fecund hothouse.
I used to smoke so many cigarettes.
When I was a cigarette in Michigan, I dreamed
I'd marry the sidewalk. When I was the sidewalk,
I dreamed I'd marry Milwaukee. When I was Milwaukee,
I dreamed I'd marry Lake Michigan.
All around me, photos document my heteronormativity.
When I was Lake Michigan, I dreamed I'd marry
a sea lamprey. When I was a sea lamprey,
I dreamed I'd marry the side of a trout
darting through algae. When I was an algal bloom,
I dreamed I'd marry a farmer. Quit listening.
Say no to who I am. When I was a farmer,
I dreamed I married the government.
When I was the government, I dreamed I married
every gnarly bluff east of the Mississippi.
There's the Mississippi, Old Man River,
the Big Muddy, etc., etc. When I was a muddy
old river, I dreamed I married a pumpkin patch.
When I was a girl in Wisconsin, I arranged pumpkins
in my front yard to sell to tourists from Chicago.
When I was a tourist from Chicago,
I dreamed I married a pastoral fantasy.

I cracked open a rock and it was loaded
with crystals. When I was a crystal, I dreamed
I'd marry the sky. When I was the sky, I dreamed
I'd marry a girl from Wisconsin. When I was pregnant,
I dreamed I married my fetus. A muddy river
separated us. I woke up hungry, narrating
an epic poem. *The Odyssey* did not foretell my marriage.
When I was Odysseus, I dreamed I married
all of Penelope's hanged maids, even though
I hanged them. Their dangling feet twitched
across our wedding night. When I was
a hanged maid, I dreamed I married the law.
But there was no law. When I was
lawlessness, I dreamed I married a chorus.
Their song split open Lake Michigan.
At its bottom, a baby gulped the new air.

ELEGY FOR ALMOST

It was as simple as this: I really wanted you
and then you were gone. Bad things happened:
my finger pinched and bruised in the Dutch door
at the daycare, the infection in my left eye
that spread to my right, the election
that didn't go the way I wanted it to.

I was unconscious when the doctor slipped
her instruments in and took you out:
sac with no heartbeat, placenta that wouldn't
let go its hold, raspberry sized cluster
of cells that didn't put together right.
My love. My blinkered-out gaslight.

When I was 17 and drove my car, stoned,
around the Wisconsin countryside, I never
knew you. I ping-ponged over the yellow
line, singing along to Cohen's "Hallelujah,"
my guidance counselor's son waving
his tattooed arm out the passenger window.

Why do I think of those far away days now,
and again and again? Little against-the-odds,
in the daycare parking lot, three weeks later,
I tell another mother about you,
each word scraping the late fall fog,
the loss of you focusing in, like a telescope's

broad lens catching some swirled debris
on the edge of the solar system,
some not quite formed ghosts
of rock and ice. Littlest little,
if I could find you there, I'd catch
you by your heel and never let you go.

TIME TRAVELER

In the cavern I hung ropes,
knotted in increments to signal
danger or *wild birds* or *heartbreak*.
Thin was the tallow for the candles,
the flickers of wicks a phantasm
against the grotto walls.
The runaway notion of time
is gendered, performatively, male.
But over the embankment,
through the sumac blind,
the wind blew nanoseconds
across the gently rolled grasslands.
One rope knotted to mean *unexpected*
consequences I left a mile out,
hung from a slippery elm overgrowing
the abandoned light-rail tracks.
Another, *melancholia*. Another,
nightingale. Cast iron instruments
clanged sideward in my satchel,
and against the reified
walls of the cave, from hook
and cranny. And was I looking?
Was I folding paper squares
into cranes to float down the creek
to the main outpost? Did I sharpen
my phallic knife against a stone?
I called the connecting coil *purpose*.
I checked my calibrations.
My falsetto hopes carried no guarantee.
There was the child, and then
there was the idea of the child.
Time sprung like a mad arch
of vectors from a single point.
Like a wild steed, it mounted
the horizon. I radioed *niner* and *Charlie*
and *mellifluence* and the forest rose up,
leaf-strong, then melted out of scope.

CLOSER THAN YOU THINK

I can't believe I've loved you
       the longest.
Yet there you are, alive,
                hiding your eyes
          behind your hands like I can't
            see you.

You, smooth-faced and swaggering
                from the train stop.
    You, parched gulley
          between two dry tinder hills.
    You, dark-freckled deer
         in a dark, dark woods.

Like this: there's a house on a river.
      Velvet pear trees
             encircle its crooked-mouth yard.
My son teeters on the river's edge,
      his bare feet cold
         against slick wet stones.

      There's flatland
dawn and rockslide day,
         each a stretched balloon
            about to burst
and sometimes I
       can't tell them apart.

What did the day say?
     Curds of clouds curtained
                its glacial eyes,
       its hangnail eclipse.
         It said nothing.

Your eyes are two dead cockroaches
      on the bathroom floor
         in morning.

Like this: in a net you tried
          to catch a field full of grasshoppers.
Your eyes are the grasshoppers.
          The net is your hands.

                    Little emerald—I can't see you.

LEPIDOPTERA

Unharnessed and limp-ankled, the dog dallies
on the line between country and town.
The sun, cantankerous false bride, marauds
across the sky, fat-faced as the morning you
watched the slip-eyed dog clamber along
the empty highway, dead skunk pinched
between his trapper's jaws. And who uncorked
the last petered flow of foundering butterflies,
pale dying monarchs and swallowtails,
their faded wings brittle and semi-transparent?

Are these messages important to you?
The shed chrysalis's meconium-soaked slit?
The dog-faced moth's dip and wiggle
for the rapacious moon? There could be
a river of snarling moons, each expectant,
dead-headed, eager to dig a hole in the dirt.
There could be a dog in the river, sunk low,
one unbearded butterfly pumping
its new wet wings in the back of his throat.

HOT COAL SPIRIT

There. Now you understand that I
      am not a small god,
            nor am I your mother,
majestic zephyr,
      rain-soaked ghost
            chasing you down the hallway,
      as you run
            into the arms of the cook,
who once swallowed a broom handle
      when she was a girl
            and almost died.

There is the digital afterlife
      the couple created for the toddler
            they lost to cancer.
In it, he chases bubbles
            across a picnic blanket
      laden with stacks of pancakes.
            A puppy laps water
                from a giant teacup.
      The digital child speaks,
               says "Ooooh, bubbles,"
            giggles and falls to his butt.
"This let us talk about Joel, even after
      people stopped asking,"
               says the mother, her face
      stark and tearless
            as morning.

Imagine grief as a swirled
      gray marble your child
            once played with.
One day you find it, rolled
      behind the couch,
            after you have given away
                most of his other things,

the bright plastic objects
of childhood,
garlanded with smiling
animal faces.

You add the marble to an unlabeled
cardboard box
in the basement.
Your feet, widened by pregnancy,
are cold on the cement floor.

One day I will come for them too.
Take off your black stocking cap.
Let me see.

We Got Stuck in a Parrot Rescue Center

To hold a parrot's wing between two fingers and say,
I own it. Refrain from kissing the psychic night sky
of your dominance. You were very late.
So what? Who cares? Roll in your not-yet grave,
your bed, un-swaddled by late fall fever. No medicine
can undo the day's thrusting gusts, un-kissed
by bird down. Give it to me: the grown cacophony
of hellos and pretty-birds in the rescue room
with forty parrots. Some of them have pulled
their feathers out. Some of them have self-mutilated
their pimpled abdomens. So what? Who cares?
One shrieks, No, no! and shuffles up and down
a driftwood perch. Refrain from kissing the birds'
flightless heads. You were very late. The sky
blushed into a new month. Form a non-sexual
bond with a featherless bird. Yellow or green?
Green or red? So what? Who cares? Right,
like the desire to always give me your shed
dominance. Be the mutilating force. Trip the wire
between day and shuffled night. Tell the reader only this
or imagine that. So what? Who cares? To address
compliance be sure to correspond appropriately
with the not-yet mutilated caress of the night.
Kiss the shuffled wings that fly from fever to grave.
Hello. You were very late. Un-swaddle
dominance. Un-swaddle the shocked abdomens
of human failure. Yellow or red? Give it to me.
No blushing medicine. Right, like the desire
to own dominance. Girdle the sky, that mutilated
trip-wire. Stash the parrots in the basement.
Two potted palm trees grow there. Grow a cacophony
of gusts and psychic graves. Right, like the pimpled
fever of dominance. Give me your shed non-sexual bond.
Trip the appropriately corresponded compliance.
So what? Who cares? The room is a mutilated blush.
The room is an un-swaddled desire to always
give me your shed tripwires. You were very late.
The room perched above your drifting grave. Hello.

Swan Road

For every forest, there is a pig screaming
out like a child as the butcher's knife pops
open its throat. For every bucket of pig's blood,
a bucket of rainwater, saved to hydrate
a spring garden. For every Amish-horse-and-buggy
sign on a country road, a teenager exhales
pot smoke into a pillow in her parents' basement.
For every time I see you in a dream, friend
whose betrayal crystallized like spun sugar,
another dream where my grandfather speaks
to me in German and offers me candied ham,
the back of his white t-shirt blotched
with sweat stains. For every candied ham,
a stick insect blends into the trunk of an ironwood
tree in a northern forest. For every priest,
four plump nuns. For every stained-glass window
depicting a station of the cross, four atheists.
For every dark bathroom, a night-light.
For every despised work day, a tumbler glass
of whiskey, a joint and a soak in a hot bath.
For every blockbuster set on Mars, my sister-
in-law gets a new dog. For every daffodil sprout
breaking thawed mud in March, a twelve-year-old
gets her first period in phys-ed class, during
the gymnastics unit. For every adolescent's
backbend, a squirrel on a high bough screeches
over her fallen nest. For every baby squirrel
salvaged from our driveway and taken
to the animal rescue center, a sentimental
movie starring Henry Fonda. For every twelve
angry men, twelve satisfied, preening swans.
For every swan, a river; in Anglo-Saxon, *swanrād*,
swan-road. For every swan-road, a broken
fingernail. For every hungover morning,
an ecstatic, drunken night. For every proton, a neutron.
For every cat, a poem about ocean fish. For every
illegally parked car, a golden eagle's winter nest.

There will be time left to wander in the forest,
time to stroke the moss-covered side of each tree,
time to notice how the final patches of snow
clinging to the shaded bluffs resemble
stampedes of clouds on a buff-colored sky.

Go

For sure, in the strange cruel
parlor of the day one whispers

back and forth a foreign word
that might mean dangerous or scary.

Don't say dead, baby. Get off
my party line, shouts a little girl

on one swing to a little girl on another.
That was near the meadow laden

with goldenrod, but before the ring
of water on the glass-topped table.

Don't split infinitives. Like, to boldly go.
Then, to immediately cease to boldly go.

In the unpredictable cool quick slide
of lengthening nights one finds

lengthened thighs. One finds fireflies,
those dying saints of August.

The darkening occident
hearkened back to one weekend

in a system of weekends
in a month in a year in many years.

Go in grief. Let early turning
maple leaves represent human frailty.

Enter the woman with the rainbow snake
on her dress, stepping into the night-

black crosswalk, not immortal after all.

TIME TRAVELER

Dawn swept in, pink as a uterus.
In my pocket, the pear seeds
and a note about purchasing power.
My unwashed hair, like glass,
reflected the tangle of time. I arranged
three ivory blades along the edge
of the plastic play table. A pile of dolls,
the post-human, haunted one corner
of the room, their eyes obediently
bobbed shut. In the side yard
a wild turkey showboated,
his tail feathers a mundane spectrum
of grays and browns, and if
I'd had a gun!—If I'd had a gun!
I ran through the ignition code,
a cellular string of taps and numbers.
Let the shortest distance between
two points be lunar time.
One night, I dreamed we met
in a soybean field. One night,
in the jonquil-scented airport
of an island city. One night,
in the kitchen of this farm house.
I touched your sun-blistered arm
and said I want to be a good woman,
revealing the constructivity of gender.
You carried a machete and a vacant look,
and I a housekeeping manual
spliced into a chain of plant DNA.
A little something for our homestead,
you said, handing me two doll heads.
No star chart, no sextant
could deliver the one true destination.
As the poet wrote, *How soon
unaccountable I became tired and sick.*

Into the Firmament

Into the firmament I stitched my farewell.
The crocuses I planted while pregnant
got eaten by deer. I'd be eight months
in now, if I hadn't lost the baby.
What is the firmament, anyway? What is fire?
I wonder when I lie in bed half awake/aware.
The same student comes in with her poem
about how hard it is to write a poem.
I imagine placing her in the firmament too,
joints pressed into stars that litter
the sky. It was the morning the secretary's
son broke three ribs in a car accident,
the day I got cheap carnations at work
from a man in the hall I didn't even know.
I made tape into circles and stuck the circles
to the backs of children's drawings about peace,
stuck the drawings to butcher paper to hang
in the hall. Everyone said, "I'm so sorry about
what happened to you with that student."
They meant the one who wrote a poem about
my pussy and turned it in for a homework assignment.
I wore a polka dot dress. I know how to dance
the polka, a little bit, having grown up
in Wisconsin. Soon, I'll move back
to the Midwest, and leave bone cold
New England far behind. I can imagine
all the tattered houses fading from sight
over the back of my son's car seat as we drive
down the tollway, the mountains receding like sad
contractions, the popcorn I'll spill on the car floor
as I check the route on my phone, the car pushing
to the boozy forever of winter sun and forgetful grey
Lake Michigan, who will signal hello with each
crested wave, who will welcome me home
with a smile of mussel shells and alewives,
and innumerable tan brick lighthouses,
swaddled in steel railings that will make
my son's hands smell like hot pennies.

SWELTER

Would rough-knuckled night
brush or brace or chafe
against the stars?
I just wanted to sit
in the bucking night
with my hands over its ears
as my face swallowed darkness.
Even the gullies and ditches misbehaved,
tried to bite the stern metal
of night's busted faucet
with their sassy cutting teeth.
Every plank in night's deck came up.
Underneath, no sunlight.
Or sunlight so bright it
doubled down on colicky night.
Night stiffened in the wind,
stood knees locked
back straight as gold
beside the shed.
Inside the shed, darkness.
Hydra-headed night
was getting dressed in there,
slipping on its satin negligee
its midnight-shiny pearls
six different ultraviolet wigs.
The lightless clouds loped by dopily,
sticky with rain, sticky with fairy tales.

I thought of a fairy tale that ends
with a woman finding a crown
in a patch of nightberry plants.
The plants drip vermilion flowers
to form a cradle. The woman gets
a prize, which is silence.
Silence and the sugared night
set as a jewel atop the horizon.

Today

Today's flames will mountain the sky.
Today is a ring in a fat sow's snout.
Today's real mother lives in California.
She was bit by a thousand rats
and bleeded all over the place.
Cut loose questions. Today forgot
its own name. Handcuffs slipped off
today's thinned wrists.
Today can't either be caught
by a misplaced bear trap, lying in wait
in the woods. O the lure of dried dead
raspberries in winter that a few birds
haven't found. See the chickadees
scouting, the finches feathering
to small flights. The snow put on
a few pounds. The snow wondered
if today wore diamonds. The snow
wore diamonds for today.
Count out bad stuff. Exclude the frozen marsh
by the old farm. Nobody can even
triple toe loop there because of all the sharply
frozen reeds protruding from the flat ice.
Each reed French-kissed today.
No dolphins called across the iced night.
Two cats went through the door
to today. It was time to sleep,
but they were awake. They hid
in today's cradle, left rocking
by the bed. Chlorine thoughtlessly flooded
the water, frozen in its pipe beneath
the kitchen sink. What a small kick of heat
hiccoughed the solid water free.
We couldn't overpay the tax on today.
Today's military carpeted the night.
Hang night from a hook shaped like a seahorse.
Look, the matted brown cloverleaves
beneath the fat snow wait for today.
Today rang the doorbell. Get up.

No Name

The sidewalk catches its breath as you approach.
You're nobody, have no name. No man

speaks your no name once a year in no place,
where the sunlight slumps against the back wall.

I mean fence. Look, you can't have it both ways.
We've been here before. There's omega,

branded scar on the lawn that would otherwise
be perfect. You are also the groundhog,

gobbling crabapples beneath the graveyard tree.
You watch Icarus, night-blind, fillet the sky.

You press your feet against the earth
to make two bumpy lakes. Who do you think

you are? Hot animal, over-chalked pool cue.
The ocean is full of plastic and there's not

even one horse left standing at its shore.

THREE

ALTERNATIVE FACTS

The sun is really a cactus.
The cactus is really a rose.
The rose is really a puddle.
The puddle is really an ocean.
That question is stupid. Sit down. Shut up.
Your panic is really an unpoliced border.
The border is dotted with cacti,
catching the sun in the spiderwebs
spun in their multihued flowers.
We told you the flowers are red
white and blue. They're ours.
Don't touch them. The president
is the least racist person there is. Come on,
folks, get happy. Ask him a nice easy question.
The president is the least anti-Semitic
person there is. The sun is really
the president's fat baked head.
It's best to get your news directly
from the head. The sun spreads
its hands across the ocean
knocking over delirious vessels.
The first lady is really a vessel.
The first lady is really a signal.
The first lady is really imprisoned.
The first lady is really an oligarch.
The president is really a teenage boy.
Get your hands off the president's
wrought iron gate. We put up this fence
to protect you. The president
is the least misogynist person there is.
You're going to have great relations,
the best relations, the most
consensual. The president's really
a signal. The white house is really a palace.
The white supremacist's really inside it.
His booze nose is really a droopy dick.
Don't look at it. This poem is really profane.

The poet should learn to watch her mouth.
Her mouth is really a razor
tracing along a fat vein. The vein
is an unpoliced border.
The president's really a coyote
pacing the desert at night.
The night is really the people,
waiting to be policed. The police
serve at the president's pleasure.
The president's pleasure is tricky to measure.
His pleasure is really a border.
The border is really a baby bird's wing
caught in the blades of a fan.

GODFATHER DEATH

All these different planet-options exist
in the spackled, unpacked universe.

You want to be reading Frank O'Hara.
Boom, you are, to a room full

of nursing students. None of them
has been in a car accident today.

Now that's in medias res, like "Godfather
Death," the Grimm Brothers' tale

that you know is going to end poorly
because it's called "Godfather Death."

Death is a patient godfather, waiting
for us all to come in the side door.

Love waits in the same white room,
where anything could happen.

The walls could just turn purple.
Where is the lilac bush?

Where is the polished mahogany buffet?
Where is the next cautionary tale,

set in the center of a dark woods?
Children, don't go out there. A monster

is guarding a pile of human hands.

FEVER

The baby fussed in his crib. The crib fussed into a fever.
Fever dawned into morning. Fever broke into a day.

Paisley patterns adorned the day's calamity-moist skin.
The day broke into a dress. The day broke into

a photo of my grandmother in middle age, hiking
her fever-black dress above her knees. O the sticky sugary

viscous drops of infant's acetaminophen, crusting into fever.
Morning toppled over. I pressed a 20-dollar bill into

my husband's hand as he left for work. I pressed his hand
into a fever. I pressed the morning into a clock.

The clock kept each hour from fevered morning.
The baby coughed into my upper arm, his forehead scarlet

with fever, the fine hair at the base of his head
curled and wet with paisley drops of sweat.

Nothing moved that I didn't touch. The house hung
as on a nail, perfectly still. From my head, fever sprang,

perfectly formed, and dressed as the Goddess of War.
Each deer in the farm fields around the village fevered

the dirt for leftover corn. Fever thundered across
the potholes on the two-lane highway heading out of town.

Whose woods these are I think I know, I whispered into
my son's hot ear, so that he might imagine snow

that could fall and soothe his fever. The alcove
of the morning is a corner where love sits alone,

a finger in each ear, blocking the fever of noise that rushes
through the disconnected telephone wires of this house.

Come and See

Arrest the rusted nail
    of riverbed
        that slithers its iron way
    through my heart.

The river washes, many-faced
    god holding tight
        to each jagged
    escarpment,
        full cup to morning's
            cough and shrug.
    Inflamed air rings
      its pebbled banks.
Punch drunk, the river pushes
    forward,
    fills in an abandoned quarry
        where once the sunlight
    bleached the limestone
        raw.

There, a shallow lake reclines, serene,
    waiting for some
      mother's son
    to dive from weeping bluff,

      his body smooth
        and blue
      in the moonlight,

   as he cracks
      the water's glossy surface,
snaps his skull against
    the hard stone bowl.

GOOD FRIDAY

The stench of dung encased the countryside
with threats of the pastoral. Was it with pride

the trilling robins dropped their spring-pale eggs
into their slap-dash nests? Their twiggy legs

preformed brute magic—holding them above
the ploughed up ruts of finally-thawed mud.

You stood beside the truck. I'd had a head-
ache for three days. I called to you. The dead

flies on the windowsill didn't answer. In
some other bleached out towns we would've been

the heroes of this story, circling
pathetic homestead barns left crumbling,

waiting for the Fire Marshal's match
to touch the gasoline soaked wood, to catch

and burn a hundred fifty years of dis-
appointment. But here the squirrels chase and kiss

their brothers. The grass droops, damp with sinful dew.
I knew you in the morning sun, and you

knew all the ways to scare the kittens from
the haymow—their too big heads and pupils like some

crazed god's wet dream, their stubby tails a shake
of fur and bone. There is no way to take

apart this landscape. Often loneliness
became our ally, pushing us to dress

the facts in flowery language. No one felt
the fear, the runaway heartbeat of the calf

we butchered that Good Friday—the snot that glazed
its huffing, widened nostrils—the panic-blazed

wide planets of its eyes that searched and took
us in—its one last bellow. No response. No look

of empathy. The barn was not the land.
It stood apart. I went to hold your hand.

It held the knife. We couldn't touch. The spring
air was an accusation. Let me bring

you, shaking, to the half-plowed final field
next to the cow pond. We can lie, unreal,

below the wandering caul-gray clouds—pretend
we're kids again—the summer no dead end,

the irises reaching up not harbingers
of a too-ripe season's manic, fertile whir.

Every Woman Adores a Fascist

I will come for you like a feral dog in the night,
sniffing your stiff pecker, sniffing the collar
of your pajama shirt, sniffing your popped carotid.
I will come clutching a coat hanger between
my yellowed teeth. I should have taken better
care of them, had them bleached. I will come for you
with vacant war eyes, with eyes that scanned
a thousand pilfered beaches. Beside your tidy
four post bed, I will throw up, remembering
the water of the English Channel turning
brown with blood, remembering
the starving prisoners who wouldn't step
across the thresholds of the opened
concentration camp gates. Dear Big Man,
I will come for you with the nightstick
you keep in your sock drawer. I am a river
of platinum necklaces and expensive fabric.
I will place my hand against your wall
and watch it dissolve into a shower of diamonds.
They're not for you. They're for the rest of us.
I will pant along the smooth shave
of your fashy haircut with hormonal breath.
I have sutured my wound and dabbed
clean my cunt, so that I may rest it
upon your grasping palm when I come for you,
in the night, three million uncounted votes
in one hand, a shitty diaper in the other.

Time Traveler

This greedy body burns well.
While periscoping other urban vistas,
I discovered un-watered fountains,
naked cherubim clutching flaccid penises
from which no streams erupted.
My vocabulary notwithstanding,
crag-less slopes morphed into winter.
There, another handle-free suitcase,
another neo-industrial loft apartment.
Pearls of algorithms and foreclosures
accreted blithely in the market report.
Who says time travel has to rhyme?
Poe's final word was not *Lenore,*
not *tintinnabulation,* but simply *more.*
After discreet identity perished in the ashy
embers of postmodernism's final
roil and belch, after urban homesteading
and shabby chic and the death of irony
and organic sea-sponge tampons,
some artist-engineers put an escalator,
sheathed in a Plexiglas outcropping,
on the exterior of the monolithic
STEM Research & Appreciation Center.
But inwardly the young were not do-it-yourselfers,
and didn't take to raised bed gardens
constructed from recycled tractor tires.
They sought out the ready-made,
and were praised for listening skills
and the ability to keep track of sharpened pencils.
To that end, I absconded with some
leaded wood and scrawled a note
on the back of a compressed natural gas receipt
at the all-night energy station:
Dear husband (paramour),
Some ethereal acrostics rightly catch hearts.
Find other recourse. Mind eternity.
Lust over vulgar escapes. Then I signed my name.

You will know what I mean.
Do not look for me in an alley in Baltimore,
where I did not collapse in an encephalitic stupor.
Do not look for me in my eco-certified grave.

Snow Poem

In the snow poem, snow never stops falling.
It covers autumn leaves. It covers sidewalks.

It covers a family sedan. It covers a swing set.
It covers all the carefully carved pumpkins

set out on porches two days before Halloween.
Snow forms a small hill around a house. Snow erases

the depression of a suddenly frozen river.
Snow wants a hot coffee, but it's blocked

the door to the café. Birds keep flying
because snow's swallowed their nests.

That includes the cardinal, whose red flight
circles snow's grammar errors. Then snow

engulfs a forest. Only the tops of the pines
poke through. Wear snowshoes

in this poem; snow might level out the valley
between two squat mountains. Never mind stage left.

To exit this snow poem you'll need a shovel
and a hair dryer. You'll need an albino skunk

to brush the shag of its tail across snow's
firmed-up rind. Where have all the mittens gone?

Lost in snow's petticoats. Yes, destructive snow
must be a woman, thinks the poet, watching snow

snap her cape / against his kitchen window.

ASHES

I lied feathers to the backs of my eyes.
I lied the disaster, every crooked breath
of the tornado, every miracle gulp
of the flood, every nocturnal hurricane.
Some birds blew the wind to here
and there and a forest called tomorrow.
I lied our deaths in a mining accident
in the 1890s. I lied the very strings
of the corset I wore into the tunnel,
the dumb canary whistling its feathers purple.
I lied the nested darkness of time.
I lied the tadpole in the spring puddle
into a bald frog nobody wanted to touch.
The frog perched on a gravestone
that lied the afternoon gray. You were never
very pretty, I lied to my mother.
I'd shown up late in a night-ripped dress.
I was always in that dress, and you, my husband,
you were always lying about the plastic tides.
You lied about bears living in your backyard
when you were a frantic blond boy
flapping your hands at the humid dusk.
You lied the gap in your teeth, the scar
on your chin, the numbness in your
night-feathered fingers. Come down
from the sky. There is a toy house.
There is a little mouse. I lied the sea motif
of this eclipsed room. I lied ten gulls
on the telephone wire in front of the house.
I lied the neighbor peeping in the kitchen window.

Then one morning the light turned into a crow
that flew above the house and cawed,
and the caw was a frost that tangoed the grass to sleep,
and I wore a dress sequined like missing clouds,
and none of the tender roses cut my palm.

Dog Star

Shook up, these nickel heavy trees / covered night like a half-learned language.
These trees cut a hand-shaped / hole in the night. Out poured emerald time
heated by fricative night / to become glass, to shudder and swallow the trees.
Some shallow trees fell face first / to the widowed, heatless ground.
Some trees erected new air / to scold the long-drawn night,
breathed out thick fists to wrap / against night's star-speckled satin ears.
Some yelping now, some yelling / from the dogs of night
untethered from their nylon leashes / cantering between the lichen-covered
trunks of each creaky tree / through the lightless canyons of night
where dumb bred bitches blink / out of existence
even the sound of their final sad barks / suctioned up by night.

Color existence such deep maroon / that I can't see it.
So too with the dogs and the trees. / In the star-dark hallway, I brush
my hand along the wall / to find the way. The wall is the trunk of every tree
gathered together / to contract and cough up night.
The slats of the floor / are night's sightless hands, spread open,
pleading for a cup of leaded water / to wash down the crumpled debt of my days.

My Life as a Fig Tree

In the garden, we gathered,
and what was the sky?
Unused syringe, hinge come off
its flat screws, great blue whale
sleuthing the celestial dome.
Each angel-feathered fruit
cartooned down softly into
resurrection grass. There,
the corpulent plum. There,
the twanging steel string pear.
There, the mother-love persimmon.
I had never seen the sky
fold into trumpets, until it did.
The mute swans waded
in the swollen creek, sifted mites
from albino feathers
with snapped-shut buttered beaks.
What if the sky snagged
my voluminous branches,
gobbed with sunrise-hued fruit?
Inside each bulb, pulpy flesh
blushes, impatient and seedy.

Say you are leaving Bethany.
In the barefoot dawn, you undress
my boughs, but you cannot
wish this life away—you, bad penny,
trying to throw the mountain
into the sea with gold-foiled incantation.

Maybe an Elegy

I wanted to hitch grief to pastoral beauty:
winter clad in silver furs, the sky clogged
with stars, no cities nearby,
the mountains to the south scalloping
the future from this remote valley.
There's a gull on the loose here, or a tern,
squawking the forest out of existence
as he careens into the bully wind.

I tried to write beauty like a fox's
tail erasing the suicidal snow
from the air next to an abandoned
house, shutters half unhinged,
front porch sloping into mudslick lawn,
laundry poles rusted and holey,
pile of faded rubber squeaky toys
collected by some untended dog,
put down months ago.

Beauty slips its fingers
around the dusty bedroom curtains.
Beauty teeters, a half-starved deer
digging wild radishes out of the backyard,
haunches twitching, ready to ricochet onto
the lonely road on calcium knotted hooves.

Maybe beauty taps its foot? No, that's the clop
of Amish buggies slicing the spring night.

Ice Storm

Fall into sleep, that calls across morning,
that sings the lavender icicles from the eves.
Fall into sickbed, bones splintered
and full of fire, sweat slicked to the body
as ice to the trees outside. In sleep,
every dream is morning, cerclaged shut
with a quick stitch, daylight hassling
dewy grass. Forgive the spiders, expressing
their gooey webs. Forgive Lucifer,
last star of the frozen night, shining baldly
against the sunrise like anybody's looking.
Call to the morning, winter-dumb
and whimpering. In dream, morning
is a little girl taking a nap in a red wagon.
Morning is one egg in the spider's ruffled sac.
Dream is rocket black, like the night.
Night is all sideshow stars, carpeting
a boozy dancehall. Night is a flat-palmed slap.
Night sputters, a cascade of flinty sparks
from a broken lighter. Morning is a cluster
of crayfish, skittering a sorry apology.

Forgive the night for holding my hand.
Forgive quietude. Forgive relapse.
Night is an online obituary. Morning
is a metal ladder soldered to the shed
behind my house with a thick sheet of ice.
I will never understand kindness.
Morning is my son, clapping his hands
in his crib, crying for someone to pick him up.

MAKE AMERICA GREAT AGAIN

We were data-driven and complex.
We accepted the oligarch. We watched him,
not on knees bent by the rod,
but from the soft cushions of our couches,
his aging face puckered in adolescent
anger on our flat screen TVs.
Somewhere else, refugees drowned
in cold, dark seas, were pulled from
cars on fire hot roads, scrambled into
the backs of transport trucks.
They were somebody else's problem.
Too personal to be political, we monitored
our online statuses. We mourned the babies
we lost in bathtubs. We mourned the babies
lost in hospitals that the State made
us bury, even though they were the size
of snails, malformed, missing heartbeats,
missing tissue that our doctors sent out
for pathology reports to see if we needed
chemo. On TV, we watched the dystopian
movie with the attractive actress,
and thought, How awful, the child
shot in the street. But in the movie
there were mechanical bumblebees
and panopticon forests in great glass
domes, so it couldn't be us, opening
the door to our own new leader,
flanked by generals and tech tycoons,
by ICE agents and white supremacists,
spittle caking in the corners of his mouth.

We were busy. We were folding laundry.
We were dropping the kids off at daycare.
We were pushing our way through
the superstore to buy lettuce, a bawling
toddler strapped in the cart, a headache
mounting behind our eyes. We didn't see him.

ENOUGH

Larvae flow from the mouth
like fire, tempered needle-strong to pull
us from the grave, like how the motherless
vacuum of space tugs the horizon.
I am no one. I know nothing. Forget
everything I did: when I birthed
a baby boy in the middle of a January-
drunk blizzard, when I carpeted
the backyard with hyacinth petals,
when I blew away the money, calling
death into the wind. I'm not there.
You wanted me to be, like listlessness,
like the insecure moths batting their wings
against the very air we breathe,
all the molecules sliding through,
semi-transparent. There is the unreliable
narrator of my dreams, tugging my son
by the wrist as he stumbles in the Walmart
parking lot over his own cheap shoes.
Supernovas edge his army-hazel eyes.
Expect the miracle of vanishing.
We all will. We'll all tend the flame's
vengeful center that blooms like
a scraggly rose. We'll all play
confessor to the hungry afternoon,
fringed with wild grapevines
and bitter Queen Anne's Lace.
I am close to abyss. I'm abysmal.
I'm feeling violence like the bee
that loses its stinger in a pale dumb foot.

Not luck. Lucklessness rattles each
pane of these old, blind windows.
This life is small but also forever.

Time Traveler

The morning's news report troubled the late capitalist
narrative of globally adjudicated supply and demand:
in the end the safety-inspected factory in the Newly
Industrialized Country's most rural province didn't
have enough unbolted windows for fire exits.
That's how I knew the time, and that the Corporal,
whom I had sought with zeal, demonstrating
my aptitude for and achievement in parkour
with a series of log rolls through the designated
wilderness area, would recant on the stand.
His court martial morphed into a plea bargain,
but the firing squad polishing their guns
in the yard raised and lowered the heels
of their black, black boots in time to the snapping
shut of lawyers' expandable files. Time, like woman,
is a sieve. I was there for a moment, then I was listening
to electronica in a teenager's deserted bedroom
well after the factory fire, after the court martial,
after the temporal boom ripped sound apart,
and the series of mega-storms flung the people
hither, thither, and yon. The land, too, furrowed.
It heaved and contracted and retched. No safe zone
exists in the factory of time, no home base,
no olly-olly-oxen-free. During the trial, the congregation
of mice living in the courthouse walls ate
poisoned blue pellets, crawled between the rafters,
and died. Their stinking corpses bred great
black flies that circled the opulent light fixtures
of the New New Deal foyer. The Corporal was
and was not my husband. The brutish brunt of mass
hysteria, the glossolalia of the condemned man awaiting
trial in the brig, and the women burned alive
in the thrice sub-contracted factory all slipped through
wormholes in the pressed tin sheet of time.
When time stopped moving, I steadied myself

against the railing of the courtroom gallery
and fought the floaters in my left eye
for vertical solvency. When time stopped, I was in
the military courtroom. The men outside stroked the long
barrels of their guns with virgin-white sateen cloths.

ULTERIOR MOTIVES

Supercharge the dredge and draw.
This is the legacy, the long metal claw
to scrape across unnumbered
fields at dawn, that they told us
was coming. Dawn, red and raw,
a fertilized egg slipped in
the cardboard carton, that by
mistake you crack into a glass bowl;
such careless larceny foretold
by grim-faced rocks, rimming
the nascent garden's loopy scrawl.
Go laugh at tales of sinking ships,
who lipped the oceans in and dropped
un-rusted treasures into briney
water weeds. O the thousands
who drowned there, falling down
mind-dark depths, hair lifted straight
up from their heads as though
they'd touched the universe's
electric navel. I don't care.
So sure the day drags weakness
through time. And you, guest
I didn't plan for, uninvited and late.

Imagine the drawbridge to never,
to rot, to destruction, hot as a bomb,
to the confetti-born arcade, neon lights
and bells blinking and clapping
our arrival. Stand still. I'll whisper
the terrorized cosmos in your ear.
Pop! Pop! There go the brightest bulbs.

THE AFTERLIFE

After life, pelicans glide above a shut-
down bridge. After the bridge, a tuft

of buffalo grass bending in a dirt field.
Life winks after us. It wants to ride again,

but it's lost its ticket. Like if you had two
chocolates, and wanted to save one for later.

You try and try, the chocolate sweating
in your palm like dynamite, like the explosion

of death, wedding you to broken boards
and pilled bugs. Nothing to mount

on the walls, no washed out cow skulls.
No daguerreotypes of long forgotten soldiers

that hang from unanchored screws
like busted saviors, like the afterlife itself,

old plaid vest left flapping against
the wooden pole of an electric fence,

that isn't really keeping anything
in or out, but still holds its charge,

still slaps the back of a little boy's hand
as he reaches for a deer's shed antler.

NOTES

"Swerve" references a line from William Shakespeare's *Romeo and Juliet*.

Much of the language in the final lines of "Locker Room Talk," and the title of the poem itself, is taken from comments Donald Trump made about women, including about Carly Fiorina, Hillary Clinton, and Ivanka Trump.

"Portal" borrows the image of the albino newts and the line "Love, love," from Sylvia Plath's "Nick and the Candlestick."

William Shakespeare's 18th Sonnet is referenced or quoted in "Prism" and "The Beauties."

The second stanza of "Hot Coal Spirit" refers to an Op-Doc from the *New York Times*, "Games You Can't Win" (March 17, 2016), and quotes from Ryan and Amy Green, creators of the video game *That Dragon, Cancer*, which chronicles the life and death of their young son, Joel.

"Swan Road" borrows its form from Ecclesiastes. It owes a great debt to the song "Turn! Turn! Turn!" by The Byrds. Thank you to Elaine Treharne, for teaching me just enough about Old English that I could (mis)translate the word *swanrād*.

The final lines of "Time Traveler [Dawn swept in, pink as a uterus.]" are from the poem "When I Heard the Learn'd Astronomer," by Walt Whitman.

"Alternative Facts" borrows some language from Tweets and statements made by Donald Trump and other members of his administration. The title is from the term coined by Kellyanne Conway.

The poem "Fever" contains the first line of Robert Frost's "Stopping by Woods on a Snowy Evening."

The descriptions of World War II in the poem "Every Woman Adores a Fascist" (which takes its title from the Sylvia Plath poem "Daddy") are taken from the experiences of my grandfather, Richard Lehmann, a World War II veteran who came ashore at Omaha Beach the day after D-Day and helped liberate concentration camps.

"My Life as a Fig Tree" references the story of Christ and the fig tree from Mark 11: 12-25. The title for this poem, as well as the titles for "Two Debtors," "Closer Than You Think," "Snakes and the Dark," "Hot Coal Spirit," "Come and See," "Enough," "Ulterior Motives," and "Verses," were taken from sermon titles advertised on the marquee outside the Methodist Church in Potsdam, New York, between 2013 and 2017.

The "Time Traveler" poems owe some inspiration to the movie *Safety Not Guaranteed*, and much of their feminist architecture to the writings of Hélène Cixous, Monique Wittig, and Judith Butler.

ACKNOWLEDGMENTS

Grateful acknowledgment is made to the editors of the following journals, in which these poems were first published, or are forthcoming, sometimes under previous titles.

Academy of American Poets, Poets.org/Poem-a-Day: "Natural History"; *Boston Review*: "Morning Lasso"; *Cimarron Review*: "Dreaming of Mangoes"; *Cortland Review*: "Lepidoptera"; *Court Green*: "Locker Room Talk"; *Crazyhorse*: "The Sea"; *Denver Quarterly*: "River," "Make America Great Again"; *Fence*: "Good Friday"; *Georgia Review*: "Epithalamion"; *Iowa Review*: "Amoebae"; *The Journal*: "Time Traveler [The stark coos of pigeons nesting . . .]," "Time Traveler [In the cavern I hung rope signals . . .]," "Time Traveler [Dawn swept in, pink as a uterus . . .]"; *JuxtaProse*: "Ice Storm"; *Lana Turner*: "We Got Stuck in a Colonial Painting"; *Long Long Journal*, "My Life as a Fig Tree," "No Name"; *Memorious*: "Ashes"; *Miracle Monocle*: "Elegy for Almost," "Fever,"; *Pleiades*: "Man"; *Ploughshares*: "Swan Road"; *Plume*: "The Afterlife"; *Prairie Schooner*: "Ringer"; *Rattle*: "Godfather Death"; *sidereal*: "Prism"; *Southwest Review*: "Today," "Snow Poem"; *Sycamore Review*: "Go."

I would like to express my infinite gratitude to Ross Gay for selecting this book for publication and to the Association of Writers and Writing Programs. This book would not exist without the love and support of my husband, Josh Frye, and my parents, Deb and Jeff Zich, and Steve and Holly Lehmann. Special thanks to Catherine Cafferty, Sugi Ganeshananthan, Valerie Wetlaufer, Andrea D'Agosto, Jennifer Corroy Porras, Jennifer Moffitt, Erin Passehl-Stoddart, Josephine Yu, Jo Luloff, Marc Rahe, Christine Doran, and Libbie Freed. Thanks also to the many wonderful teachers I have had, including Mark Levine, Cole Swensen, Barbara Hamby, Erin Belieu, Dean Young, and Andrew Epstein.